U.S. Department of Justice
Office of Justice Programs
Bureau of Justice Statistics

====== SPECIAL REPORT ======

NOVEMBER 2014

NCJ 248339

Crimes Against the Elderly, 2003–2013

Rachel E. Morgan, Ph.D., *BJS Statistician*, and Britney J. Mason, *BJS Intern*

For the period 2003–13, elderly persons age 65 or older experienced nonfatal violent crime victimizations at lower rates (3.6 victimizations per 1,000 persons age 65 or older) than younger persons ages 12 to 24 (49.9 per 1,000), persons ages 25 to 49 (27.6 per 1,000), and persons ages 50 to 64 (15.2 per 1,000) (figure 1). Nonfatal violent crime includes rape or sexual assault, robbery, aggravated assault, and simple assault. Each year, the elderly accounted for approximately 2% of violence and 2% of serious violence, which equals 136,720 violent crimes and 47,640 serious violent crimes. However, the elderly made up about 21% of the population age 12 or older during this time period. The rate of property crime was also lower compared to younger persons.

This report uses data from the National Crime Victimization Survey (NCVS) to provide detailed information on nonfatal violent victimization and property victimization against the elderly, including victim and incident characteristics. Findings in this report are also supplemented by data from the 2012 Identity Theft Supplement (ITS) to the NCVS. In addition, the primary source of information on homicides was obtained from mortality data based on death certificates in the National Vital Statistics System of the National Center for Health Statistics (NCHS), Centers for Disease Control

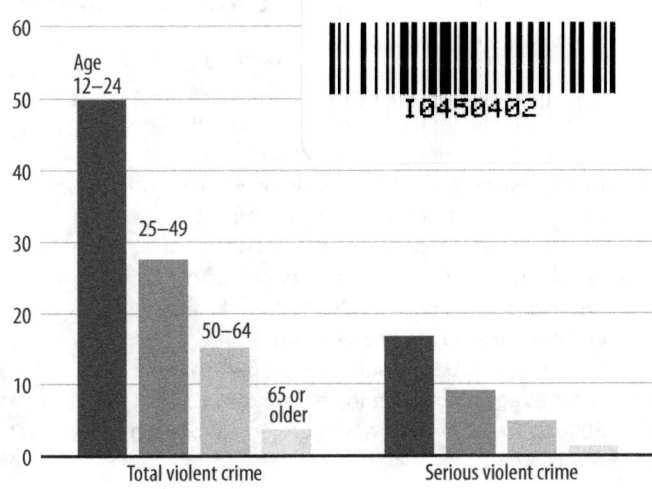

FIGURE 1

Rate of violent victimization, by type of crime and age of victim, 2003–2013

Rate per 1,000 persons

Note: See table 2 for estimates and appendix table 1 for standard errors.
Source: Bureau of Justice Statistics, National Crime Victimization Survey, 2003–2013.

HIGHLIGHTS

This report describes crimes against persons age 65 or older, by victim and incident characteristics. Data are from the National Crime Victimization Survey (NCVS), the Centers for Disease Control and Prevention's (CDC) Web-based Injury Statistics Query and Reporting System (WISQARS), and the U.S. Census Bureau. In 2003–13—

- The rates of nonfatal violent crime (3.6 per 1,000 persons) and property crime (72 3 per 1,000) against elderly persons were lower than those of younger persons.

- The ratio of the estimates of property crime to violent crime was higher for the elderly (13 to 1) than for younger persons ages 25 to 49 (3 to 1) and persons ages 50 to 64 (5 to 1).

- Elderly homicide rates declined 44%, from 3.7 homicides per 100,000 persons in 1993 to 2.1 per 100,000 in 2011.

- Persons age 65 or older experienced more incidents of identity theft (5.0%) than persons ages 16 to 24 (3.8%), but less than persons ages 25 to 49 (7.9%) and ages 50 to 64 (7.8%).

- Among elderly violent crime victims, about 59% reported being victimized at or near their home.

- A smaller percentage of elderly victims (18%) suffered an injury during the incident, compared to victims ages 12 to 24 (30%) and ages 25 to 49 (25%).

- The elderly (56%) reported incidents of violent crime to police more than persons ages 12 to 24 (38%). No differences were detected with the elderly and other age groups.

- About 11% of elderly victims of violent crime received assistance from victim service agencies.

and Prevention's (CDC) Web-based Injury Statistics Query and Reporting System (WISQARS). These mortality data include causes of death reported by attending physicians, medical examiners, and coroners, and demographic information about decedents reported by funeral directors who obtain information from family members and other informants. The NCHS collects, compiles, verifies, and prepares these data for release to the public.

In this report, elderly persons are defined as persons age 65 or older. This definition is consistent with definitions of elderly used by other federal governmental agencies, such as the U.S. Census Bureau (see figure 2). Comparison age groups include persons ages 12 to 24, 25 to 49, and 50 to 64.

Trend estimates from the NCVS are based on 2-year rolling averages centered on the most recent year. For example, estimates reported for 1994 represent the average estimates for 1993 and 1994. For ease of discussion, the report refers to all 2-year estimates by the most recent year. Other data in this report focus on the most recent 11-year aggregate period from 2003 through 2013, referred to throughout the report as 2003–13. Both approaches—using rolling averages and aggregating years—increase the reliability and stability of estimates and facilitate comparisons of detailed victimization characteristics.

Growth of the elderly population in the United States

According to the U.S. Census Bureau, the large increases in the elderly population that have occurred since 1990 are projected to continue through 2020. As many Baby Boomers are currently reaching age 65, the elderly population will continue to grow and remain an important part of the total U S. population. In 2010, about 40 3 million persons were age 65 or older, an increase of 5.3 million since 2000 when the elderly population totaled about 35 million (figure 2). Among the total U.S. population, the percentage of persons age 65 or older increased from 12.4% in 2000 to 13.0% in 2010, and is projected to reach 16.8% by 2020.

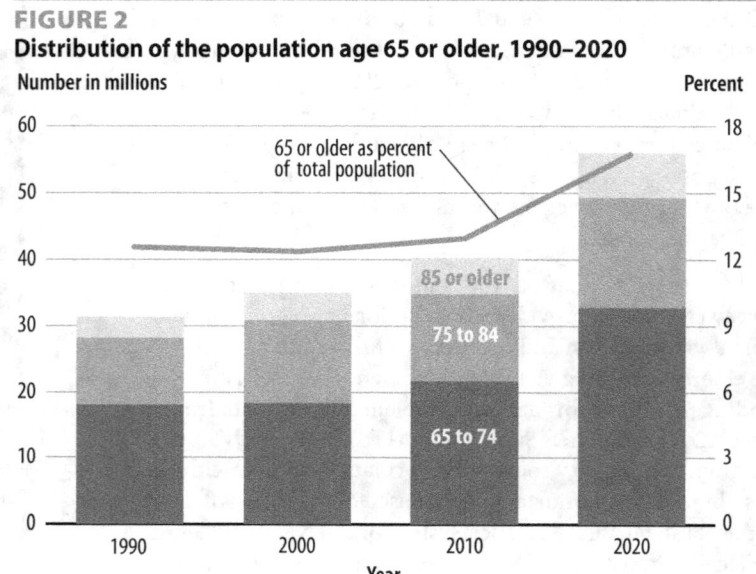

FIGURE 2
Distribution of the population age 65 or older, 1990–2020

Note: See appendix table 2 for estimates.

Source: Bureau of Justice Statistics, based on data from the U.S. Census Bureau, *65+ in the United States: 2010*, 2014.

Elderly persons had lower rates of property crime than younger persons

Like violent crime, the elderly population had lower rates of property crime compared to younger persons from 2003 to 2013. Households headed by persons age 65 or older (72.3 per 1,000 households) experienced property crime at a rate about a quarter of that for households headed by persons age 24 or younger (262.0 per 1,000) (table 1). Property crime includes household burglary, motor vehicle theft, and theft. The elderly experienced theft (51.8 per 1,000 households) more than any other type of property crime.

During 2003–13, the elderly experienced 1,796,740 property crimes annually, compared to 136,720 violent crimes annually (table 2). About 93% of all crime experienced by the elderly was property crime. The ratio of property crime to violent crime for the elderly was higher than for younger persons. In 2003–13, 13 property crimes were committed against the elderly for every violent crime committed against the elderly. In comparison, persons ages 25 to 49 experienced three property crimes for every violent crime, and persons ages 50 to 64 experienced five property crimes for every violent crime.

TABLE 1
Number and rate of property victimization, by type of crime and age of head of household, 2003–2013

Type of crime	Average annual property victimizations					Rate per 1,000 households				
	Total	24 or younger	25–49	50–64	65 or older	Total	24 or younger	25–49	50–64	65 or older
Total property crime	18,060,340	2,031,930	9,924,460	4,307,210	1,796,740	149.7	262.0	177.1	134.6	72.3
Household burglary	3,545,610	433,410	1,823,110	846,700	442,390	29.4	55.9	32.5	26.4	17.8
Motor vehicle theft	833,920	108,780	468,220	189,590	67,330	6.9	14.0	8.4	5.9	2.7
Theft	13,680,810	1,489,740	7,633,140	3,270,920	1,287,020	113.4	192.1	136.2	102.2	51.8

Note: See appendix table 3 for standard errors.
Source: Bureau of Justice Statistics, National Crime Victimization Survey, 2003–2013.

TABLE 2
Number and rate of violent victimization, by type of crime and age of victim, 2003–2013

Type of crime	Average annual violent victimizations					Rate per 1,000 persons				
	Total	12–24	25–49	50–64	65 or older	Total	12–24	25–49	50–64	65 or older
Total violent crime	6,579,800	2,709,260	2,899,310	834,510	136,720	26.1	49.9	27.6	15.2	3.6
Serious violent crime	2,170,980	912,640	947,510	263,190	47,640	8.6	16.8	9.0	4.8	1.3
Rape/sexual assault	301,430	138,480	125,940	29,740	7,260 !	1.2	2.6	1.2	0.5	0.2
Robbery	693,630	281,860	298,620	90,850	22,310	2.8	5.2	2.8	1.7	0.6
Aggravated assault	1,175,920	492,300	522,950	142,600	18,070	4.7	9.1	5.0	2.6	0.5
Simple assault	4,408,820	1,796,620	1,951,790	571,320	89,090	17.5	33.1	18.6	10.4	2.4

Note: See appendix table 1 for standard errors.
! Interpret with caution. Estimate based on 10 or fewer sample cases, or coefficient of variation is greater than 50%.
Source: Bureau of Justice Statistics, National Crime Victimization Survey, 2003–2013.

The National Crime Victimization Survey (NCVS)

The NCVS collects information on nonfatal crimes reported and not reported to the police against persons age 12 or older from a nationally representative sample of U.S. households. It produces national rates and levels of violent and property victimization, as well as information on the characteristics of crimes and victims, and the consequences of victimization. The NCVS is based on interviews with victims, it does not measure homicide.

This report examines violent crimes and property crimes. Violent crime includes rape or sexual assault, robbery, aggravated assault, and simple assault. The Bureau of Justice Statistics (BJS) classifies rape, sexual assault, robbery, and aggravated assault as serious violent crimes. Property crime includes burglary, motor vehicle theft, and other theft. The survey also measures personal larceny, which includes pickpocketing and purse snatching. For additional estimates not included in this report, see the NCVS Victimization Analysis Tool (NVAT) on the BJS website.

Victimization is the basic unit of analysis used throughout this report. Victimization is a crime as it affects one person or household. For personal crimes, the number of victimizations is equal to the number of victims present during a criminal incident. The number of victimizations may be greater than the number of incidents because more than one person may be victimized during an incident. Each crime against a household is counted as having a single victim, the affected household. The victimization rate is a measure of the occurrence of victimizations among a specified population group. For personal crimes, this is based on the number of victimizations per 1,000 residents age 12 or older. For household crimes, the victimization rate is calculated using the number of incidents per 1,000 households.

The NCVS is administered to persons age 12 or older from a nationally representative sample of households in the United States. It excludes violence against children age 11 or younger. The sample includes persons living in group quarters, such as dormitories, rooming houses, and religious group dwellings, but excludes persons living in military barracks and institutional settings, such as correctional or hospital facilities, and persons who are homeless.

The nonfatal violent crime rate for the elderly declined 41% from 1994 to 2013

From 1994 to 2013, the rate of nonfatal violent crime for all age groups decreased (figure 3). Overall, the rate of violent crime against persons age 65 or older declined 41%, from 7.4 victimizations per 1,000 persons in 1994 to 4.4 per 1,000 in 2013. Violent crime committed against the elderly declined at a slower rate than violent crime committed against persons ages 12 to 24 and ages 25 to 49. Since 2003, rates of violent crime have increased 27% for the elderly population and 9% for persons ages 50 to 64. Rates of nonfatal violent crime for persons ages 12 to 24 declined 37% and persons ages 25 to 49 declined 9% from 2003 to 2013. However, the elderly continue to have low violent crime rates compared to other age groups.

Elderly homicide rates were lower than homicide rates for all other ages from 1993 to 2011

From 1993 to 2011 (most recent data available), homicide rates decreased for all age groups (figure 4). The homicide rates for the elderly declined 44%, compared to a decline of 55% for persons ages 12 to 24, 42% for persons ages 25 to 49, and 36% for persons ages 50 to 64. The elderly rate declined from about 3.7 homicides per 100,000 persons in 1993 to 2.1 homicides per 100,000 persons in 2011. Similar to nonfatal violent crime, homicide rates for persons age 65 or older were consistently lower than all other age groups across this period.

FIGURE 3
Rate of violent victimization, by age of victim, 1993–2013

Rate per 1,000 persons

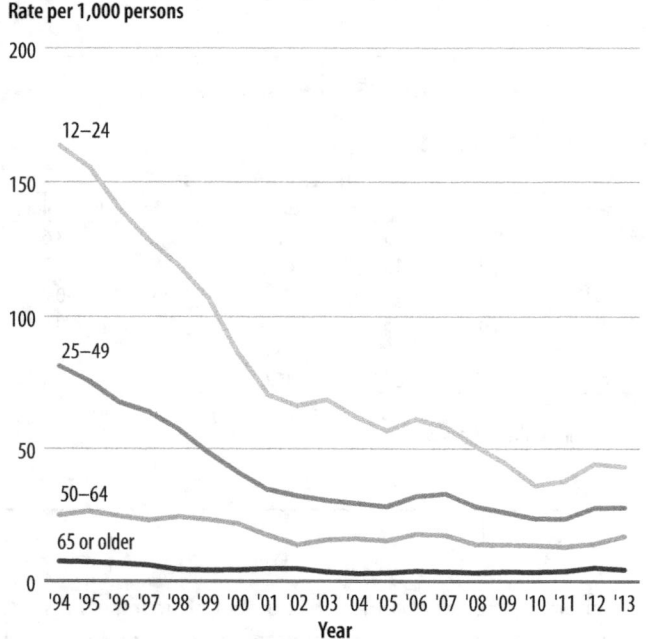

Note: Data are based on 2-year rolling averages centered on the most recent year beginning in 1993. See appendix table 4 for rates and standard errors.
Source: Bureau of Justice Statistics, National Crime Victimization Survey, 1993–2013.

FIGURE 4
Rate of homicide, by age of victim, 1993–2011

Rate per 100,000 persons

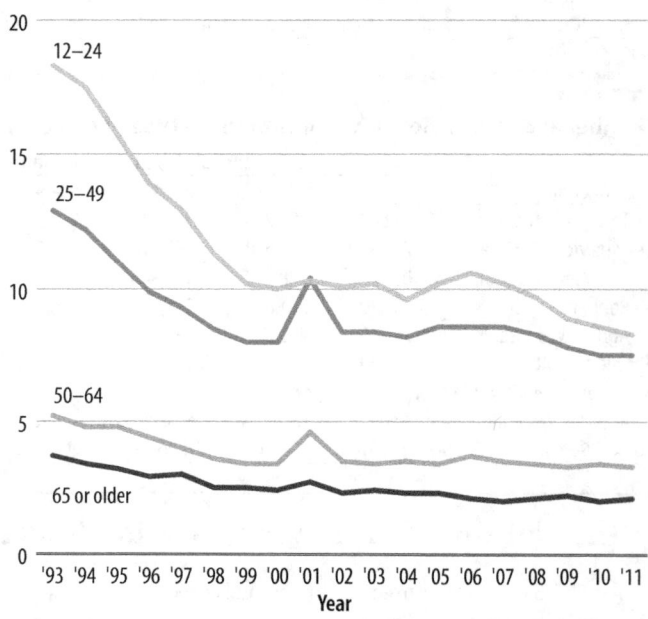

Note: The homicide estimates that occurred as a result of the events of September 11, 2001, are included in the number of total homicides. Excludes homicides due to legal intervention and operations of war. See appendix table 5 for rates.
Source: Bureau of Justice Statistics, based on data from the National Center for Injury Prevention and Control, Web-based Injury Statistics Query and Reporting System (WISQARS), 1993–2011.

Similar to the overall decline in homicide, the firearm homicide rate for the elderly population decreased by 41% from 1993 to 2011 (figure 5). Persons ages 25 to 49 and ages 50 to 64 also experienced a 41% decline in homicide. The firearm homicide rate for the elderly declined from about 1.4 per 100,000 persons age 65 or older in 1993 to 0.8 per 100,000 in 2011. Since 2003, the rates of firearm homicide increased for the elderly population (up 9%) and for persons ages 50 to 64 (up 1%). However, the elderly continued to have relatively low rates overall.

From 1993 to 2011, the rates of nonfirearm homicide decreased for all age groups. The rates for the elderly declined by 46%, compared to a decline of 51% for persons ages 12 to 24, 44% for persons ages 25 to 49, and 28% for persons ages 50 to 64 (figure 6). The rate for the elderly declined from about 2.2 per 100,000 in 1993 to 1.2 per 100,000 in 2011.

FIGURE 5

Rate of firearm homicide, by age of victim, 1993–2011

Rate per 100,000 persons

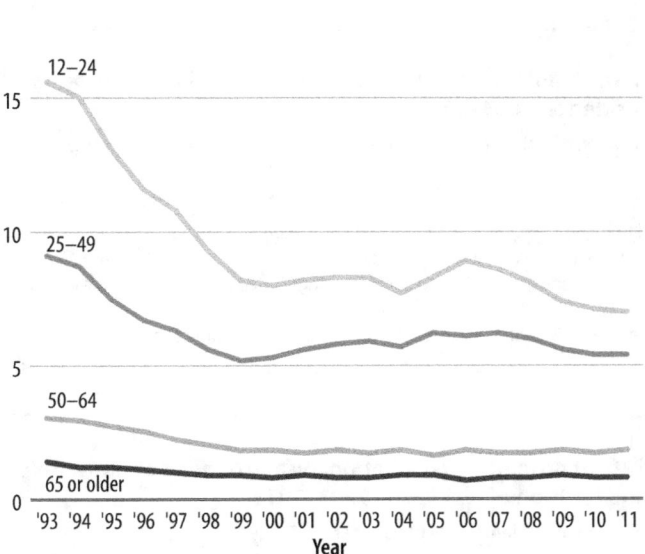

Note: Excludes homicides due to legal interventions and operations of war. See appendix table 6 for rates.

Source: Bureau of Justice Statistics, based on data from the National Center for Injury Prevention and Control, Web-based Injury Statistics Query and Reporting System (WISQARS), 1993–2011.

FIGURE 6

Rate of nonfirearm homicide, by age of victim, 1993–2011

Rate per 100,000 persons

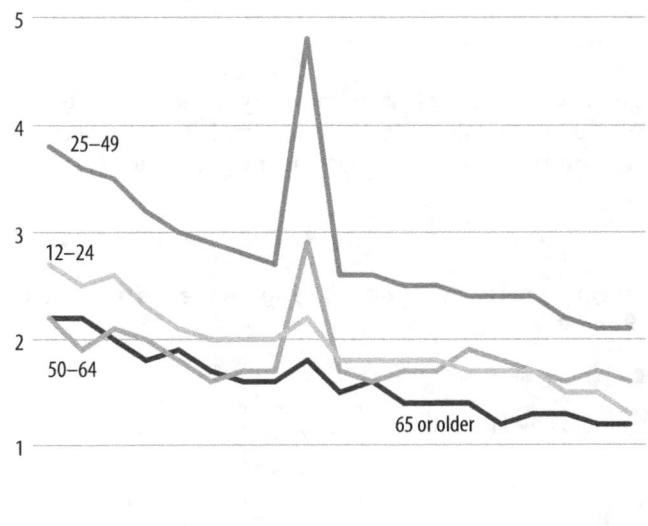

Note: The homicide estimates that occurred as a result of the events of September 11, 2001, are included in the number of nonfirearm homicides. Excludes homicides from legal intervention and operations of war. See appendix table 7 for rates.

Source: Bureau of Justice Statistics, based on data from the National Center for Injury Prevention and Control, Web-based Injury Statistics Query and Reporting System (WISQARS), 1993–2011.

Property crime committed against the elderly decreased by 48% from 1994 to 2013

Similar to violent crime, the rate of property crime for all age groups declined from 1994 to 2013 (figure 7). During this period, property crime decreased by 48% for the elderly, compared to declines of 55% for persons ages 12 to 24, 60% for persons ages 25 to 49, and 52% for persons ages 50 to 64. The elderly rate declined from about 141.0 victimizations per 1,000 households in 1994 to 73.9 per 1,000 households in 2013. The rates for the elderly were lower than all other age groups across this period. Property crime committed against the elderly declined by 50% from 2003 to 2013.

Elderly victims of violent and property crimes most often lived in urban areas

Elderly victims of violent and property crimes most often resided in urban areas. In 2003–13, elderly persons living in urban areas experienced violent crime at a rate of 5.1 per 1,000 persons age 65 or older, while elderly persons living in suburban (3.2 per 1,000) and rural (2.8 per 1,000) areas experienced violent crime at lower rates (table 3). Similarly, elderly victims living in urban areas had a higher rate of property crime (88.7 per 1,000 households) compared to those living in suburban areas (65.2 per 1,000 households) and rural areas (66.6 per 1,000 households) (table 4).

In 2003–13, about 59% of nonfatal violent crime against persons age 65 or older occurred at or near their homes, 6% occurred at or near a friend, neighbor, or relative's home, and about 35% occurred at other locations, including commercial places, parking lots or garages, schools, open areas, and public transportation (table 5). A greater percentage of victimization against the elderly compared to all other age groups occurred at or near their homes.

FIGURE 7
Rate of property victimization, by age of head of household, 1993–2013

Rate per 1,000 households

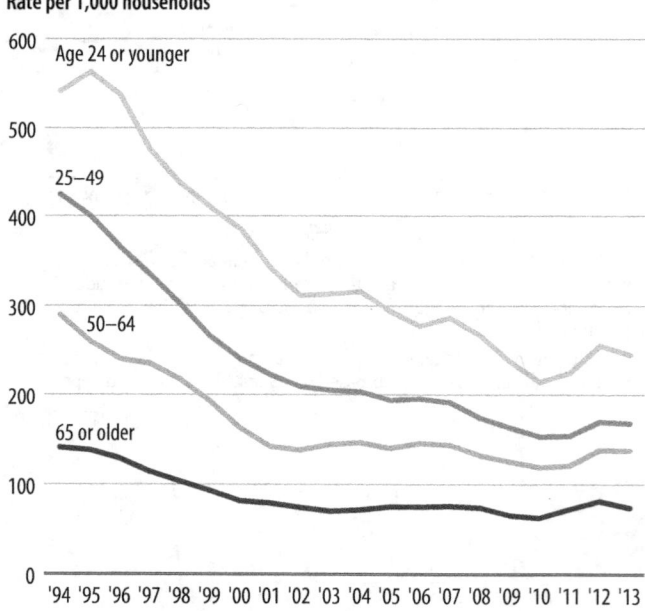

Note: Data are based on 2-year rolling averages centered on the most recent year beginning in 1993. See appendix table 8 for rates and standard errors.
Source: Bureau of Justice Statistics, National Crime Victimization Survey, 1993–2013.

TABLE 3
Rate of violent victimization, by age of victim and location of residence, 2003–2013

Location of residence	12–24	25–49	50–64	65 or older
Urban	54.7	32.6	21.5	5.1
Suburban	46.0	24.1	13.0	3.2
Rural	51.9	28.7	12.3	2.8

Note: Victimization rates are per 1,000 persons age 12 or older. Violent crime includes rape or sexual assault, robbery, aggravated assault, and simple assault. See appendix table 9 for standard errors.
Source: Bureau of Justice Statistics, National Crime Victimization Survey, 2003–2013.

TABLE 4
Rate of property victimization, by age of head of household and location of residence, 2003–2013

Location of residence	24 or younger	25–49	50–64	65 or older
Urban	281.9	211.3	168.4	88.7
Suburban	235.3	157.5	122.8	65.2
Rural	265.1	166.6	114.6	66.6

Note: Victimization rates are per 1,000 households. Property crime includes household burglary, motor vehicle theft, and theft. See appendix table 10 for standard errors.
Source: Bureau of Justice Statistics, National Crime Victimization Survey, 2003–2013.

TABLE 5
Location of violent victimization, by age of victim, 2003–2013

Location of crime	12–24	25–49	50–64	65 or older
Total	100%	100%	100%	100%
At or near victim's home	25.4	41.1	43.5	59.3
At or near friend, neighbor, or relative's home	11.3	5.9	5.5	6.0
Other location*	63.3	53.1	51.0	34.7
Average annual violent victimizations	2,709,260	2,899,310	834,510	136,720

*Includes commercial places, parking lots or garages, schools, open areas, public transportation, and other locations. See appendix table 11 for standard errors.
Source: Bureau of Justice Statistics, National Crime Victimization Survey, 2003–2013.

About 2.1 million elderly persons were victims of identity theft in 2012

Identity theft victims are defined as persons age 16 or older who experienced one or more of the following incidents:

- Unauthorized use or attempted use of an existing account, such as credit or debit card, checking, savings, telephone, online, or insurance account (referred to as fraud or misuse of an existing account).

- Unauthorized use or attempted use of personal information to open a new account, such as a credit or debit card, telephone, checking, savings, loan, or mortgage account (referred to as fraud or misuse of a new account).

- Misuse of personal information for a fraudulent purpose, such as getting medical care, a job, or government benefits; renting an apartment or house; or providing false information to law enforcement when charged with a crime or traffic violation (referred to as fraud or misuse of personal information).

Approximately 2.1 million persons age 65 or older (5%) were victims of one or more incidents of identity theft in 2012 (table 6). Among elderly identity theft victims, existing credit card (3.2%) or bank accounts (1.4%) were the most common types of misused information. This distribution was similar across age groups. Generally, persons age 65 or older experienced more incidents of identity theft (5.0%) than persons ages 16 to 24 (3.8%), but fewer than persons ages 25 to 49 (7.9%) and ages 50 to 64 (7.8%).

TABLE 6
Persons age 16 or older who experienced at least one identity theft incident in the past 12 months, by type of theft and age of victim, 2012

Type of theft	Number of victims				Percent of all persons			
	16–24	25–49	50–64	65 or older	16–24	25–69	50–64	65 or older
Total identity theft	1,501,630	8,208,300	4,739,430	2,131,120	3.8%	7.9%	7.8%	5.0%
Existing account	1,482,150	8,397,140	4,865,740	2,120,530	3.8%	8.1%	8.0%	5.0%
Credit card	335,670	3,399,560	2,590,400	1,372,830	0.9	3.3	4.2	3.2
Bank	953,640	4,062,720	1,853,250	601,080	2.4	3.9	3.0	1.4
Other	192,840	934,860	422,090	146,620	0.5	0.9	0.7	0.3
New account	126,930	520,310	315,660	162,250	0.3%	0.5%	0.5%	0.4%
Personal information	78,730	463,290	211,360	80,200	0.2%	0.4%	0.3%	0.2%
Multiple types	122,030	657,970	330,810	141,230	0.3%	0.6%	0.5%	0.3%
Existing account[a]	86,800	433,670	211,580	92,610	0.2	0.4	0.3	0.2
Other[b]	35,220	224,300	119,230	48,620	0.1	0.2	0.2	0.1

Note: Detail may not sum to total due to rounding and multiple responses. See appendix table 12 for standard errors.

[a]Includes victims who experienced two or more of the following: unauthorized use of a credit card, bank account, or other existing account.

[b]Includes victims who experienced two or more of the following: unauthorized use of an existing account, misuse of personal information to open a new account, or misuse of personal information for other fraudulent purposes.

Source: Bureau of Justice Statistics, National Crime Victimization Survey, Identity Theft Supplement, 2012.

Domestic violence was a smaller percentage of violent crimes committed against elderly persons than against persons ages 25 to 49 and ages 50 to 64

From 2003–13, the elderly (49%) were equally likely to know their offenders as persons ages 25 to 49 and ages 50 to 64, but were less likely than persons ages 12 to 24 (57%) (table 7). About 43% of violent victimizations against the elderly were committed by strangers.

A smaller percentage of violent crimes committed against persons age 65 or older (14%) were crimes of domestic violence, compared to persons ages 25 to 49 (26%) and ages 50 to 64 (20%). Domestic violence includes rape, sexual assault, robbery, and aggravated and simple assault committed by intimate partners, immediate family members, or other relatives. As with any source of information, there are limitations with the current data that should be recognized. Because the nature of the victim–offender relationship is defined by the victim, the characteristics of intimate partner violence in this report may differ based on how the respondent perceived their relationship with the offender. To some victims, intimate relationships with offenders may be primarily restricted to current or former boyfriends or girlfriends. Others may describe those offenders as friends or acquaintances rather than boyfriends or girlfriends.

While 43% of violent crimes against the elderly were committed by a stranger, the elderly accounted for 2% of all stranger crime (table 8). The majority of stranger crime was committed against persons ages 12 to 24 (37%) and persons ages 25 to 49 (48%). From 2003–13, the percentage of victimizations that involved an intimate partner was lower for the elderly (1%) than for persons ages 12 to 24 (28%) and persons ages 25 to 49 (62%), and lower than persons ages 50 to 64 (8%). The percentage of victimizations committed by immediate family members was lower for the elderly (2%) compared to all other age groups. Elderly victims accounted for 2.1% of violent crime, 2.4% of crime committed by strangers, and 1.4% of domestic violence that occurred each year.

TABLE 7

Violent victimization, by age of victim and victim–offender relationship, 2003–2013

Victim–offender relationship	12–24	25–49	50–64	65 or older
Total	100%	100%	100%	100%
Known	57.2%	50.6%	52.1%	48.8%
Domestic	16.4	26.0	19.9	14.3
Intimate partner[a]	9.9	20.4	9.6	6.1
Immediate family	4.2	3.5	7.3	4.6
Other relative	2.2	2.1	3.0	3.6
Well-known/casual acquaintance	40.8	24.6	32.3	34.5
Stranger	34.0%	41.2%	39.8%	43.4%
Unknown[b]	8.8%	8.1%	8.1%	7.8%
Average annual violent victimizations	2,709,260	2,899,310	834,510	136,720

Note: Detail may not sum to total due to rounding. See appendix table 13 for standard errors.
[a]Includes current or former spouses, boyfriends, and girlfriends.
[b]Includes unknown victim–offender relationships and unknown number of offenders.
Source: Bureau of Justice Statistics, National Crime Victimization Survey, 2003–2013.

TABLE 8

Percent of violent victimization, by victim–offender relationship and age of victim, 2003–2013

Victim–offender relationship	Total	12–24	25–49	50–64	65 or older
Total	100%	41.2%	44.1%	12.7%	2.1%
Known	100%	44.0	41.7	12.4	1.9
Domestic	100%	32.1	54.5	12.0	1.4
Intimate partner[a]	100%	28.4	62.3	8.5	0.9
Immediate family	100%	40.4	36.0	21.3	2.2
Other relative	100%	39.8	40.7	16.2	3.2
Well-known/casual acquaintance	100%	51.8	33.4	12.6	2.2
Stranger	100%	36.7	47.7	13.2	2.4
Unknown[b]	100%	43.1	42.8	12.2	1.9

Note: Detail may not sum to total due to rounding. See appendix table 14 for standard errors.
[a]Includes current or former spouses, boyfriends, and girlfriends.
[b]Includes unknown victim–offender relationships and unknown number of offenders.
Source: Bureau of Justice Statistics, National Crime Victimization Survey, 2003–2013.

Single elderly persons living without children had higher rates of victimization compared to married elderly persons living without children

In 2003–13, the rate of violent victimizations against elderly males (4.2 per 1,000 males age 65 or older) was slightly higher than the rate for elderly females (3.2 per 1,000 females) (table 9). There were no statistically significant differences in rates of violent crime among the elderly by race.

Among the elderly population and other age groups, rates of violent victimization varied by the victim's marital status. Persons age 65 or older who were married (2.6 per 1,000 persons) or widowed (2.3 per 1,000 persons) were the least likely to be victims of violent crime. Elderly persons who were separated (19.6 per 1,000 persons) or divorced (10.8 per 1,000 persons) were the most likely to be victimized. Since the NCVS reflects a respondent's marital status at the time of the interview, it is not possible to determine whether a person was separated or divorced at the time of the victimization or whether separation or divorce followed the violence.

Single elderly victims living without children (5.2 victimizations per 1,000 persons) were victimized at higher rates than married elderly victims living without children (2.4 per 1,000).

Elderly persons who rented their living quarters had more than double the rate of violent crime (7.3 victimizations per 1,000 persons) than elderly persons who either owned or were buying their home (3.0 victimizations per 1,000).

TABLE 9

Rate of violent victimization, by age of victim and victim characteristics, 2003–2013

Demographic characteristic	12–24	25–49	50–64	65 or older
Sex				
Male	53.8	28.7	16.4	4.2
Female	45.8	26.5	14.2	3.2
Race/Hispanic origin				
White[a]	53.4	28.9	15.1	3.4
Black[a]	53.7	31.2	18.1	5.0
Hispanic/Latino	39.4	19.2	12.3	3.5
Other race[a,b]	24.0	19.4	10.8	3.6!
Two or more races[a]	99.0	92.7	53.4	11.4!
Marital status				
Never married	49.7	35.7	24.1	6.6
Married	34.9	16.2	9.4	2.6
Widowed	31.9!	48.5	18.8	2.3
Divorced	208.5	54.7	30.6	10.8
Separated	219.5	101.1	40.8	19.6
Household composition				
Single, no children	63.6	43.6	29.2	5.2
Married, no children	31.6	15.0	8.4	2.4
With children[c]	50.2	22.6	18.3	1.0!
Other[d]	49.4	32.6	14.9	4.0
Household ownership status				
Owned	41.3	20.0	11.6	3.0
Rented	61.8	41.8	31.4	7.3
No cash rent	83.9	44.7	33.2	3.3!

Note: Victimization rates are per 1,000 persons age 12 or older. See appendix table 15 for standard errors.

! Interpret with caution. Estimate based on 10 or fewer sample cases, or coefficient of variation is greater than 50%.

[a]Excludes persons of Hispanic or Latino origin.

[b]Includes American Indian, Alaska Native, Asian, Native Hawaiian, and other Pacific Islander.

[c]Single or married with children.

[d]Both single and married adults living with other adults (relatives or nonrelatives), both with and without children. This includes grandparents and grandchildren living in the same household.

Source: Bureau of Justice Statistics, National Crime Victimization Survey, 2003–2013.

There were no statistically significant differences between violent crime rates for elderly persons with a disability and elderly persons without a disability

The NCVS defines disability as the product of interactions among individual's bodies; their physical, emotional, and mental health; and the physical and social environment in which they live, work, or play. Disability exists where this interaction results in limitations of activities and restrictions to full participation at school, work, home, or in the community. Disabilities are classified according to six limitations: hearing, vision, cognitive, ambulatory, self-care, and independent living.*

Over the 5-year period from 2008 to 2012, persons age 65 or older who had disabilities experienced 284,040 nonfatal violent crimes (table 10). However, there were no differences in the rate of violence for persons age 65 or older with a disability compared to persons age 65 or older without a disability.

TABLE 10
Number and rate of violent victimization for persons age 65 or older, by type of crime and victim's disability status, 2008–2012

Type of crime	Number of violent victimizations		Rate per 1,000 persons	
	With disabilities	Without disabilities	With disabilities	Without disabilities
Total violent crime	284,040	512,920	3.9	4.1
Serious violent crime	109,220	125,410	1.5	1.0
Rape/sexual assault	52,370 !	11,500 !	0.7 !	0.1 !
Robbery	32,230	62,120	0.4	0.5
Aggravated assault	24,620	51,790	0.3	0.4
Simple assault	174,830	387,500	2.4	3.1

Note: Based on the noninstitutionalized U.S. residential population age 65 or older. Numbers rounded to the nearest hundred. See appendix table 16 for standard errors.

! Interpret with caution. Estimate based on 10 or fewer sample cases, or coefficient of variation is greater than 50%.

Source: Bureau of Justice Statistics, National Crime Victimization Survey, 2008–2012.

*Crimes Against Persons with Disabilities, 2009-2012 – Statistical Tables, NCJ 244525, BJS web, February 2014.

Elderly persons who were not employed were more likely to experience violent and property crime victimization than elderly persons who were employed

Employment status affects both nonfatal violent and property crime rates for persons age 65 or older. For both types of crime, persons who were not employed were more likely to be victimized than employed persons. In 2003–13, the rate of violent crime against elderly persons who were not employed or were retired (2.8 per 1,000) was 9 times higher than the rate for elderly persons who were employed (0.3 per 1,000) (table 11). The rate of property crime against persons age 65 or older who were not employed or were retired (53.5 per 1,000 persons) was 12 times higher than the rate for persons age 65 or older who were employed (4.3 per 1,000).

TABLE 11
Rates of violent and property victimization, by employment status and age, 2003–2013

Employment status and age	Violent crime[a]	Property crime[b]
Employed		
12–64	6.0	24.7
65 or older	0.3	4.3
Not employed/retired		
12–64	12.9	54.9
65 or older	2.8	53.5

Note: Victimization rates are per 1,000 persons for violent crime and per 1,000 households for property crime. See appendix table 17 for standard errors.

[a]Includes rape or sexual assault, robbery, aggravated assault, and simple assault. Age is by victim for violent crime.

[b]Includes household burglary, motor vehicle theft, and theft. Age is by head of household for property crime.

Source: Bureau of Justice Statistics, National Crime Victimization Survey, 2003–2013.

Elderly violent crime victims were as likely to encounter a weapon as persons of other ages

Though the elderly were victimized at a lower rate, when victimized they were as likely to encounter a weapon and a firearm as persons of other ages. About 1 in 5 (20%) violent victimizations against the elderly involved a weapon (i.e., a firearm, knife, or other object) (table 12). A firearm was used in about 8% of violent crimes against elderly victims. Knives were used in about 4% of violent victimizations against persons 65 or older, while about 6% involved other types of weapons.

Of the elderly who were injured during violent crime incidents, most reported bruises or cuts

A smaller percentage of elderly victims suffered an injury (18%), compared to younger victims ages 12 to 24 (30%) and ages 25 to 49 (25%) (table 13). Among the elderly who were injured, most reported bruises or cuts. Approximately 45% of elderly victims who were injured received some type of treatment. Of those treated, about 55% of persons age 65 or older received treatment in a doctor's office, hospital emergency room, or overnight in a hospital. About 45% of injured elderly victims were treated at the scene of the crime, in their home, the home of a neighbor or friend, or other location. No statistically significant differences were detected among age groups in the percentage treated for injury or location of treatment.

TABLE 12

Percent of violent victimizations involving a weapon, by age of victim, 2003–2013

Type of weapon	12–24	25–49	50–64	65 or older
Total	100%	100%	100%	100%
No weapon	72.6%	70.2%	69.9%	69.3%
Weapon	21.5%	22.4%	21.0%	19.5%
Firearm	6.2	7.7	7.0	7.6
Knife	6.4	5.9	5.6	4.3
Other	7.2	7.1	6.9	6.2
Type unknown	1.6	1.7	1.5	1.4 !
Don't know	5.9%	7.5%	9.0%	11.1%
Average annual violent victimizations	2,709,260	2,899,310	834,510	136,720

Note: Detail may not sum to total due to rounding. See appendix table 18 for standard errors.

! Interpret with caution. Estimate based on 10 or fewer sample cases, or coefficient of variation is greater than 50%.

Source: Bureau of Justice Statistics, National Crime Victimization Survey, 2003–2013.

TABLE 13

Percent of violent victimizations resulting in injury and medical treatment, by age of victim, 2003–2013

Type of injury and treatment	12–24	25–49	50–64	65 or older
Total	100%	100%	100%	100%
Not injured	70.5	74.9	79.6	82.1
Injured	29.5	25.1	20.4	17.9
Serious injuries[a]	5.8	5.2	4.4	2.9
Bruises or cuts	24.7	21.1	16.3	14.2
Other injuries	3.4	2.5	2.5	3.7
Treatment for injury[b]	100%	100%	100%	100%
No treatment	62.1	56.4	59.0	54.6
Any treatment	37.8	43.4	40.1	45.4
Treatment setting[c]	100%	100%	100%	100%
At the scene/home of victim, neighbor, or friend/ other location	38.7	44.5	36.8	45.4
In doctor's office/hospital emergency room/ overnight at hospital	61.3	55.5	63.2	54.6

Note: Detail may not sum to total due to rounding. See appendix table 19 for standard errors.

[a]Includes sexual violence injuries, gunshot wounds, knife wounds, internal injuries, unconsciousness, and broken bones.

[b]Includes only victims who were injured.

[c]Includes only victims who were injured and received treatment.

Source: Bureau of Justice Statistics, National Crime Victimization Survey, 2003–2013.

The elderly reported 56% of violent crime and 38% of property crime to police

In 2003–13, the elderly (56%) were more likely to report violent crime to the police than persons ages 12 to 24 (38%) (table 14). There were no differences in reporting between the elderly and persons of other ages. A slightly higher percentage of elderly serious violent crime victims (64%) reported the incident to the police, compared to elderly victims of simple assault (52%). Persons age 65 or older reported about 38% of property crime to police. In comparison to household burglary (50%) and motor vehicle theft (83%), theft (32%) was the property crime least likely to be reported to police by persons age 65 or older. This was also true for the other age groups.

About 21% of elderly victims of serious violent crime sought assistance from victim service agencies

Victim service agencies are publicly or privately funded organizations that provide victims with support and services to aid their physical and emotional recovery, offer protection from future victimizations, guide them through the criminal justice system process, and assist them in obtaining restitution. Similar to other age groups, about 1 in 10 (11%) elderly violent crime victims received assistance from victim service agencies (table 15). Serious violent crime victims age 65 or older received more assistance (21%), compared to persons ages 12 to 24 (10%) and ages 50 to 64 (10%) and slightly more assistance than persons ages 25 to 49 (13%).

TABLE 14
Percentage of victimizations reported to police, by type of crime and age of victim, 2003–2013

Type of crime	12–24	25–49	50–64	65 or older
Violent crime[a]	38.0%	53.5%	50.5%	56.2%
Serious violent crime[b]	48.0	63.9	58.2	64.3
Rape/sexual assault	30.9	43.5	25.4	28.0 !
Robbery	52.8	64.8	61.2	76.1
Aggravated assault	50.0	68.2	63.1	64.3
Simple assault	32.9	48.5	47.0	51.8
Property crime[c]	36.9%	38.2%	36.6%	38.3%
Household burglary	52.3	56.2	51.7	50.1
Motor vehicle theft	78.6	82.8	79.0	83.5
Theft	29.3	31.1	30.3	31.9

Note: See appendix table 20 for standard errors.

! Interpret with caution. Estimate based on 10 or fewer sample cases or coefficient of variation is greater than 50%.

[a]Includes rape or sexual assault, robbery, aggravated assault, and simple assault. Age is by victim for violent crime.

[b]Includes rape or sexual assault, robbery, and aggravated assault.

[c]Includes household burglary, motor vehicle theft, and theft. Age is by head of household for property crime.

Source: Bureau of Justice Statistics, National Crime Victimization Survey, 2003–2013.

TABLE 15
Violent crime victims who received assistance from a victim service agency, by age of victim, 2003–2013

Type of crime	12–24	25–49	50–64	65 or older
Total	7.7%	11.2%	7.9%	10.8%
Serious violent crime*	9.7	13.4	10.1	21.5
Simple assault	6.6	10.2	6.9	5.1 !

Note: See appendix table 21 for standard errors.

! Interpret with caution. Estimate based on 10 or fewer sample cases or coefficient of variation is greater than 50%.

*Includes rape or sexual assault, robbery, and aggravated assault.

Source: Bureau of Justice Statistics, National Crime Victimization Survey, 2003–2013.

Methodology

Estimates in this report are based primarily on data from the Bureau of Justice Statistics' (BJS) National Crime Victimization Survey (NCVS), including data from the Identity Theft Supplement (ITS). Additional data come from the Centers for Disease Control and Prevention's (CDC) Web-based Injury Statistics Query and Reporting System (WISQARS).

The NCVS is an annual data collection conducted by the U.S. Census Bureau for BJS. The NCVS is a self-report survey in which interviewed persons are asked about the number and characteristics of victimizations experienced during the prior 6 months. The NCVS collects information on nonfatal personal crimes (rape or sexual assault, robbery, aggravated and simple assault, and personal larceny) and household property crimes (burglary, motor vehicle theft, and other theft) both reported and not reported to police. In addition to providing annual level and change estimates on criminal victimization, the NCVS is the primary source of information on the nature of criminal victimization incidents.

Survey respondents provide information about themselves (e.g., age, sex, race and Hispanic origin, marital status, education level, and income) and whether they experienced a victimization. For each victimization incident, information is collected about the offender (e.g., age, sex, race and Hispanic origin, and victim–offender relationship), characteristics of the crime (including time and place of occurrence, use of weapons, nature of injury, and economic consequences), whether the crime was reported to police, reasons the crime was or was not reported, and experiences with the criminal justice system.

The NCVS is administered to persons age 12 or older from a nationally representative sample of households in the United States. The NCVS defines a household as a group of members who all reside at a sampled address. Persons are considered household members when the sampled address is their usual place of residence at the time of the interview and when they have no usual place of residence elsewhere. Once selected, households remain in the sample for 3 years, and eligible persons in these households are interviewed every 6 months either in person or over the phone for a total of seven interviews.

Generally, all first interviews are conducted in person. New households rotate into the sample on an ongoing basis to replace outgoing households that have been in the sample for the 3-year period. The sample includes persons living in group quarters, such as dormitories, rooming houses, and religious group dwellings, and excludes persons living in military barracks and institutional settings, such as correctional or hospital facilities, and persons who are homeless. (For more information, see the Survey Methodology for *Criminal Victimization in the United States, 2008*, NCJ 231173, BJS web, May 2011.)

The NCVS was designed to measure the incidence of criminal victimization against the U.S. civilian household population, excluding persons who live in institutions and the homeless. In this report, institutions refer to adult correctional facilities, juvenile facilities, nursing facilities or skilled nursing facilities, in-patient hospice facilities, residential schools for people with disabilities, and hospitals with patients who have no usual home elsewhere. The measures of crime against persons age 65 or older cover only elderly persons who are living among the general population in household settings. Subsequently, there is some coverage error in using just the noninstitutionalized population. For example, according to the U.S. Census, about 3.1% of the elderly population were living in nursing homes in 2010. Because persons in these facilities would not be covered in the NCVS, estimates of violence against these persons are not counted. The lack of information from the institutions will result in an undercount of violence against persons age 65 or older. Additionally, some care should be taken when comparing victimization rates within the elderly population. Data from the U.S. Census Bureau indicate that an estimated 0.9% of the U.S. population ages 65 to 74 lived in a nursing home in 2010, compared to 3.2% of the population ages 75 to 84 and 11.2% of the population age 85 or older.

In 2013, 90,630 households and about 160,040 persons age 12 or older were interviewed for the NCVS. Each household was interviewed twice during the year. The response rate was 84% for households and 88% for eligible persons. Victimizations that occurred outside of the United States were excluded from this report. In 2013, less than 1% of the unweighted victimizations occurred outside of the United States and were excluded from the analyses.

Estimates in this report use data primarily from the 1993 to 2013 NCVS data files weighted to produce annual estimates for persons age 12 or older living in U.S. households. Because the NCVS relies on a sample rather than a census of the entire U.S. population, weights are designed to inflate sample point estimates to known population totals and to compensate for survey nonresponse and other aspects of the sample design.

The NCVS data files include both household and person weights. The household weight is commonly used to calculate estimates of property crimes, such as motor vehicle theft or burglary, which are identified with the household. Person weights provide an estimate of the population represented by each person in the sample. Person weights are most frequently used to compute estimates of crime victimizations of persons in the total population. After proper adjustment, both household and person weights are also used to form the denominator in calculations of crime rates.

The victimization weights used in this analysis account for the number of persons present during an incident and for repeat victims of series incidents. The weight counts series incidents as the actual number of incidents reported by the victim, up to a maximum of 10 incidents. Series victimizations are victimizations that are similar in type but occur with such frequency that a victim is unable to recall each individual event or to describe each event in detail. Survey procedures allow NCVS interviewers to identify and classify these similar victimizations as series victimizations and collect detailed information on only the most recent incident in the series. In 2013, about 1% of all victimizations and 4% of all violent victimizations were series incidents. Weighting series incidents as the number of incidents up to a maximum of 10 produces more reliable estimates of crime levels, while the cap at 10 minimizes the effect of extreme outliers on the rates. Additional information on the series enumeration is detailed in *Methods for Counting High Frequency Repeat Victimizations in the National Crime Victimization Survey* (NCJ 237308, BJS website) April 2012.

Standard error computations

When national estimates are derived from a sample, as with the NCVS, caution must be taken when comparing one estimate to another estimate or when comparing estimates over time. Although one estimate may be larger than another, estimates based on a sample have some degree of sampling error. The sampling error of an estimate depends on several factors, including the amount of variation in the responses, and the size of the sample. When the sampling error around an estimate is taken into account, the estimates that appear different may not be statistically different.

One measure of the sampling error associated with an estimate is the standard error. The standard error can vary from one estimate to the next. Generally, an estimate with a small standard error provides a more reliable approximation of the true value than an estimate with a large standard error. Estimates with relatively large standard errors are associated with less precision and reliability and should be interpreted with caution.

To generate standard errors around numbers and estimates from the NCVS, the Census Bureau produced generalized variance function (GVF) parameters for BJS. The GVFs take into account aspects of the NCVS complex sample design and represent the curve fitted to a selection of individual standard errors based on the Jackknife Repeated Replication technique. The GVF parameters were used to generate standard errors for each point estimate (i.e., counts, percentages, and rates) in this report.

BJS conducted tests to determine whether differences in estimated numbers and percentages in this report were statistically significant once sampling error was taken into account. Using statistical programs developed specifically for the NCVS, all comparisons in the text were tested for significance. The Student's t-statistic was the primary test procedure, which tests the difference between two sample estimates.

Data users can use the estimates and the standard errors of the estimates provided in this report to generate a confidence interval around the estimate as a measure of the margin of error. The following example illustrates how standard errors can be used to generate confidence intervals:

In 2003–13, according to the NCVS, the rate of nonfatal violent crime against persons age 65 or older was 3.6 per 1,000 (see table 2). Using the GVFs, it was determined that the estimate has a standard error of 0.3 (see appendix table 1). A confidence interval around the estimate was generated by multiplying +/- 1.96 (the t-score of a normal, two-tailed distribution that excludes 2.5% at either end of the distribution). Therefore, the 95% confidence interval around the 3.6 estimate from 2013 is 3.6 +/- (0.3 X 1.96) or (3.0 to 4.3). In other words, if different samples using the same procedure were taken from the U.S. population in 2003–13, 95% of the time the rate of nonfatal violent crime against persons age 65 or older would be between 3.0 and 4.3 per 1,000 persons age 65 or older.

In this report, BJS also calculated a coefficient of variation (CV) for all estimates, representing the ratio of the standard error to the estimate. CVs provide a measure of reliability and a means to compare the precision of estimates across measures with differing levels or metrics. In cases where the CV was greater than 50%, or the unweighted sample had 10 or fewer cases, the estimate was noted with a "!" symbol. (Interpret data with caution. Estimate based on 10 or fewer sample cases, or the coefficient of variation is greater than 50%.)

Data Collection for Disability Statistics

In 2007, the NCVS adopted questions from the U.S. Census Bureau's American Community Survey (ACS) to measure the rate of victimization against people with disabilities. The NCVS does not identify persons in the general population with disabilities. The ACS Subcommittee on Disability Questions developed the disability questions based on questions used in the 2000 Decennial Census and earlier versions of the ACS. The questions identify persons who may require assistance to maintain their independence, be at risk for discrimination, or lack opportunities available to the general population because of limitations related to a prolonged (6 months or longer) sensory, physical, mental, or emotional condition. More information about the ACS and the disability questions is available on the U.S. Census Bureau website at http://www.census.gov/acs/www/.

Changes to the disability questions in the NCVS and ACS in 2008

In 2008, the U.S. Census Bureau changed some of the disability questions on the ACS. The question about sensory disability was separated into two questions about blindness and deafness, and the questions about physical disability were asked only about serious difficulty walking or climbing stairs. Also, questions on employment disability and going outside of the home were eliminated in 2008. Census Bureau analysis of 2007 and 2008 ACS disability data revealed significant conceptual and measurement differences between the 2007 and 2008 disability questions. The Census Bureau concluded that data users should not compare the 2007 estimates of the population with disabilities and those of later years. Because the 2007 and 2008 NCVS disability questions mirrored the ACS, estimates of victimization of people with disabilities from the 2007 and 2008 NCVS should not be compared. As a result, the 2007 disability data are not presented in this report. Further explanation about incomparability of the 2007 and 2008 ACS disability data is available at http://www.census.gov/acs/www/Downloads/methodology/content_test/P4_Disability.pdf.

Definitions of disability types

Disabilities are classified according to six limitations: hearing, vision, cognitive, ambulatory, self-care, and independent living.

- Hearing limitation entails deafness or serious difficulty hearing.

- Vision limitation is blindness or serious difficulty seeing, even when wearing glasses.

- Cognitive limitation includes serious difficulty in concentrating, remembering, or making decisions because of a physical, mental, or emotional condition.

- Ambulatory limitation is difficulty walking or climbing stairs.

- Self-care limitation is a condition that causes difficulty dressing or bathing.

- Independent living limitation is a physical, mental, or emotional condition that impedes doing errands alone, such as visiting a doctor or shopping.

Data Collection for Identity Theft Statistics

From January 1, 2012, through June 30, 2012, the Identity Theft Supplement (ITS) was administered at the end of the NCVS interview to persons age 16 or older in sampled NCVS households. Proxy responders and those who completed the NCVS interview in a language other than English were not eligible to receive the ITS. All NCVS and ITS interviews were conducted in a computer-assisted personal interviewing (CAPI) environment. Interviews were conducted by telephone or by personal visit. A final sample size of 69,814 of the original NCVS-eligible respondents completed the ITS questionnaire, resulting in a response rate of 91.9%. The combined overall NCVS-ITS unit response rate for NCVS households, NCVS persons, and ITS persons was 68.2%. Because of the level of nonresponse, a bias analysis was conducted. To the extent that those who responded to the survey and those who did not differ in important ways, there is potential for bias in estimates from the survey data. However, the result of the nonresponse bias analysis suggested that there was little or no bias of substantive importance due to nonresponse in the ITS estimates.

The ITS collected individual data on the prevalence of and victim response to the attempted or successful misuse of an existing account, misuse of personal information to open a new account, or misuse of personal information for other fraudulent purposes. Respondents were asked whether they had experienced any of these types of misuse during the 12 months prior to the interview. For example, persons interviewed in July 2012 were asked about identity theft incidents that occurred between July 2011 and June 2012. To simplify the discussion of the findings, this report refers to all identity theft experienced during the 12 months prior to the interviews as occurring in 2012.

Persons who reported one or more incidents of identity theft during 2012 were then asked more detailed questions about the incident and response to the incident, such as how the identity theft was discovered; financial, credit, and other problems resulting from the incident; time spent resolving problems associated with the theft; and reporting to police and credit bureaus. For most sections of the survey instrument, victims who experienced more than one incident during the 12-month reference period were asked to think about only the most recent incident when answering questions. Victims who experienced multiple incidents of identity theft during the year were asked to report on the total financial losses suffered as a result of all incidents.

Both victims and nonvictims were also asked a series of questions about experiences with identity theft outside of the 12-month reference period and about measures taken to avoid or minimize the risk of becoming an identity theft victim.

For more information on crimes against the elderly, see previous BJS publications:

- *Crimes Against Persons Age 65 or Older, 1992–1997*, NCJ 176352, January 2000
- *Crimes Against Persons Age 65 or Older, 1993–2002*, NCJ 206154, January 2005
- *Violent Crimes Against the Elderly Reported by Law Enforcement in Michigan, 2005–2009*, NCJ 238546, June 2012

Standard errors for figure 1 and table 2: Number and rate of violent victimization, by type of crime and age of victim, 2003–2013

Type of crime	Average annual violent victimizations					Rate per 1,000 persons age 12 or older				
	Total	12–24	25–49	50–64	65 or older	Total	12–24	25–49	50–64	65 or older
Total violent crime	369,424	203,451	212,820	94,794	31,657	0.7	1.6	0.9	0.7	0.3
Serious violent crime	175,752	100,327	102,747	46,578	17,404	0.3	0.8	0.4	0.3	0.2
Rape/sexual assault	39,769	25,099	23,755	10,569	4,973	0.1	0.2	0.1	0.1	0.0
Robbery	76,903	44,237	45,801	22,808	10,470	0.1	0.3	0.2	0.2	0.1
Aggravated assault	86,600	50,041	51,945	23,816	7,528	0.2	0.4	0.2	0.2	0.1
Simple assault	271,615	149,665	158,004	72,063	23,857	0.5	1.2	0.7	0.6	0.2

Source: Bureau of Justice Statistics, National Crime Victimization Survey, 2003–2013.

Estimates for figure 2: Distribution of the population age 65 or older, 1990–2020

Age	1990	2000	2010	2020
Total (in millions)	31.2	35.0	40.3	56.0
65–74	18.1	18.4	21.7	32.8
75–84	10.1	12.4	13.1	16.5
85 or older	3.1	4.2	5.5	6.7
65 or older as percent of total population	12.6%	12.4%	13.0%	16.8%

Source: Bureau of Justice Statistics, based on data from the U.S. Census Bureau, *65+ in the United States: 2010*, 2014.

Standard errors for table 1: Number and rate of property victimization, by type of crime and age of head of household, 2003–2013

Type of crime	Average annual property victimizations					Rate per 1,000 households				
	Total	24 or younger	25–49	50–64	65 or older	Total	24 or younger	25–49	50–64	65 or older
Total property crime	438,364	122,129	306,298	187,619	113,963	1.4	4.7	2.0	2.1	1.6
Household burglary	151,881	47,337	104,068	68,033	47,861	0.5	2.0	0.7	0.7	0.7
Motor vehicle theft	57,807	19,558	42,276	26,150	15,254	0.2	0.8	0.3	0.3	0.2
Theft	341,242	94,391	241,152	147,258	87,015	1.1	3.8	1.6	1.6	1.2

Source: Bureau of Justice Statistics, National Crime Victimization Survey, 2003–2013.

APPENDIX TABLE 4
Rates and standard errors for figure 3: Rate of violent victimization, by age of victim, 1993–2013

Year	Rate per 1,000 persons				Standard errors			
	12–24	25–49	50–64	65 or older	12–24	25–49	50–64	65 or older
1994	163.4	80.9	24.7	7.4	7.4	3.9	2.7	1.3
1995	155.4	75.1	26.1	7.1	6.2	3.2	2.3	1.1
1996	139.9	67.4	24.3	6.7	6.1	3.2	2.3	1.0
1997	128.3	63.7	22.8	6.0	6.5	3.4	2.4	1.1
1998	118.9	57.2	24.1	4.4	7.5	3.9	3.0	1.1
1999	106.9	48.6	23.1	4.1	6.7	3.3	2.7	1.0
2000	86.1	41.0	21.6	4.3	6.0	3.0	2.6	1.0
2001	70.2	34.4	17.3	4.7	5.0	2.6	2.1	1.0
2002	66.1	32.0	13.6	4.7	5.3	2.7	2.0	1.1
2003	68.3	30.3	15.5	3.4	5.4	2.6	2.2	0.9
2004	61.7	29.1	15.9	2.8	4.7	2.4	2.0	0.8
2005	56.6	27.9	15.2	3.1	4.2	2.2	1.9	0.8
2006	61.1	31.8	17.6	3.8	4.1	2.2	1.9	0.8
2007	57.8	32.7	17.1	3.5	4.0	2.3	1.8	0.7
2008	51.0	28.0	13.8	3.2	4.0	2.2	1.7	0.8
2009	44.4	25.8	13.7	3.6	4.3	2.5	2.0	1.0
2010	35.9	23.4	13.4	3.4	3.7	2.3	1.9	0.9
2011	37.6	23.3	12.9	3.7	3.5	2.1	1.6	0.8
2012	44.2	27.5	14.0	5.1	3.3	2.0	1.5	0.9
2013	43.2	27.6	16.8	4.4	2.4	1.5	1.3	0.7

Source: Bureau of Justice Statistics, National Crime Victimization Survey, 1993–2013.

APPENDIX TABLE 5
Rates for figure 4: Rate of homicide, by age of victim, 1993–2011

Year	12–24	25–49	50–64	65 or older
1993	18.3	12.9	5.2	3.7
1994	17.5	12.2	4.8	3.4
1995	15.7	11.0	4.8	3.2
1996	13.9	9.9	4.4	2.9
1997	12.9	9.3	4.0	3.0
1998	11.3	8.5	3.6	2.5
1999	10.2	8.0	3.4	2.5
2000	10.0	8.0	3.4	2.4
2001	10.3	10.4	4.6	2.7
2002	10.1	8.4	3.5	2.3
2003	10.2	8.4	3.4	2.4
2004	9.6	8.2	3.5	2.3
2005	10.2	8.6	3.4	2.3
2006	10.6	8.6	3.7	2.1
2007	10.2	8.6	3.5	2.0
2008	9.7	8.3	3.4	2.1
2009	8.9	7.8	3.3	2.2
2010	8.6	7.5	3.4	2.0
2011	8.3	7.5	3.3	2.1

Note: Rates are per 100,000 persons.
Source: Bureau of Justice Statistics, based on data from the National Center for Injury Prevention and Control, Web-based Injury Statistics Query and Reporting System (WISQARS), 1993–2011.

APPENDIX TABLE 6
Rates for figure 5: Rate of firearm homicide, by age of victim, 1993–2011

Year	12–24	25–49	50–64	65 or older
1993	15.6	9.1	3.0	1.4
1994	15.0	8.7	2.9	1.2
1995	13.1	7.5	2.7	1.2
1996	11.6	6.7	2.5	1.1
1997	10.8	6.3	2.2	1.0
1998	9.3	5.6	2.0	0.9
1999	8.2	5.2	1.8	0.9
2000	8.0	5.3	1.8	0.8
2001	8.2	5.6	1.7	0.9
2002	8.3	5.8	1.8	0.8
2003	8.3	5.9	1.7	0.8
2004	7.7	5.7	1.8	0.9
2005	8.3	6.2	1.6	0.9
2006	8.9	6.1	1.8	0.7
2007	8.6	6.2	1.7	0.8
2008	8.1	6.0	1.7	0.8
2009	7.4	5.6	1.8	0.9
2010	7.1	5.4	1.7	0.8
2011	7.0	5.4	1.8	0.8

Note: Rates are per 100,000 persons.
Source: Bureau of Justice Statistics, based on data from the National Center for Injury Prevention and Control, Web-based Injury Statistics Query and Reporting System (WISQARS), 1993–2011.

APPENDIX TABLE 7
Rates for figure 6: Rate of nonfirearm homicide, by age of victim, 1993–2011

Year	12–24	25–49	50–64	65 or older
1993	2.7	3.8	2.2	2.2
1994	2.5	3.6	1.9	2.2
1995	2.6	3.5	2.1	2.0
1996	2.3	3.2	2.0	1.8
1997	2.1	3.0	1.8	1.9
1998	2.0	2.9	1.6	1.7
1999	2.0	2.8	1.7	1.6
2000	2.0	2.7	1.7	1.6
2001	2.2	4.8	2.9	1.8
2002	1.8	2.6	1.7	1.5
2003	1.8	2.6	1.6	1.6
2004	1.8	2.5	1.7	1.4
2005	1.8	2.5	1.7	1.4
2006	1.7	2.4	1.9	1.4
2007	1.7	2.4	1.8	1.2
2008	1.7	2.4	1.7	1.3
2009	1.5	2.2	1.6	1.3
2010	1.5	2.1	1.7	1.2
2011	1.3	2.1	1.6	1.2

Note: Rates are per 100,000 persons.

Source: Bureau of Justice Statistics, based on data from the National Center for Injury Prevention and Control, Web-based Injury Statistics Query and Reporting System (WISQARS), 1993–2011.

APPENDIX TABLE 8
Rates and standard errors for figure 7: Rate of property victimization, by age of head of household, 1993–2013

Year	Rate per 1,000 households				Standard errors			
	24 or younger	25–49	50–64	65 or older	24 or younger	25–49	50–64	65 or older
1994	541.4	424.4	289.5	141.0	15.7	7.6	9.2	6.4
1995	563.1	400.1	260.0	138.1	12.2	5.8	6.8	4.9
1996	537.4	365.9	240.4	128.6	13.6	6.0	7.1	5.2
1997	475.9	336.0	235.0	114.0	13.4	5.9	7.0	4.8
1998	437.5	302.2	217.7	103.3	17.4	7.7	8.9	6.1
1999	409.7	265.6	192.5	92.9	17.3	7.2	8.3	5.8
2000	385.6	240.3	162.7	81.6	16.7	7.3	7.7	5.3
2001	343.6	223.0	142.4	79.3	13.0	5.7	5.8	4.3
2002	311.9	209.4	138.2	74.5	11.9	4.8	5.1	3.9
2003	313.6	205.2	144.3	70.1	14.8	6.3	6.7	4.7
2004	315.8	203.2	146.4	71.7	14.8	6.3	6.6	4.8
2005	294.0	193.7	140.3	75.0	11.3	4.3	4.8	3.8
2006	277.1	195.5	146.0	75.0	10.8	3.9	4.5	3.7
2007	286.4	191.1	143.8	75.8	13.5	5.2	5.7	4.5
2008	266.5	173.9	132.4	73.9	13.2	5.2	5.6	4.5
2009	237.3	162.8	125.2	65.4	12.5	4.9	5.3	4.1
2010	214.5	153.0	119.0	62.6	11.9	4.6	4.9	4.0
2011	224.5	153.7	120.6	72.4	12.1	4.8	5.1	4.3
2012	254.8	169.7	138.1	81.5	13.1	5.3	5.6	4.7
2013	244.7	167.7	137.9	73.9	8.2	3.2	3.5	2.8

Source: Bureau of Justice Statistics, National Crime Victimization Survey, 1993–2013.

APPENDIX TABLE 9
Standard errors for table 3: Rate of violent victimization, by age of victim and location of residence, 2003–2013

Location of residence	12–24	25–49	50–64	65 or older
Urban	2.4	1.4	1.4	0.6
Suburban	1.9	1.0	0.8	0.4
Rural	2.9	1.7	1.1	0.5

Source: Bureau of Justice Statistics, National Crime Victimization Survey, 2003–2013.

APPENDIX TABLE 11
Standard errors for table 5: Location of violent victimization, by age of victim, 2003–2013

Location of crime	12–24	25–49	50–64	65 or older
At or near victim's home	1.0%	1.2%	1.8%	3.7%
At or near friend, neighbor, or relative's home	0.7	0.5	0.7	1.6
Other location	1.3	1.3	1.9	3.4
Average annual violent victimizations	203,451	212,820	94,794	31,657

Source: Bureau of Justice Statistics, National Crime Victimization Survey, 2003–2013.

APPENDIX TABLE 10
Standard errors for table 4: Rate of property victimization, by age of head of household and location of residence, 2003–2013

Location of residence	24 or younger	25–49	50–64	65 or older
Urban	6.6	3.1	3.6	2.9
Suburban	6.8	2.3	2.5	2.0
Rural	10.1	3.8	3.6	2.9

Source: Bureau of Justice Statistics, National Crime Victimization Survey, 2003–2013.

APPENDIX TABLE 12
Standard errors for table 6: Persons age 16 or older who experienced at least one identity theft incident in the past 12 months, by type of theft and age of victim, 2012

Type of theft	Estimate				Percent			
	16–24	25–49	50–64	65 or older	16–24	25–49	50–64	65 or older
Total identity theft	154,243	475,443	330,527	194,365	0.4%	0.4%	0.5%	0.4%
Existing account	152,923	482,612	336,354	193,724	0.4%	0.4%	0.5%	0.4%
Credit card	58,768	265,013	221,219	145,410	0.1	0.2	0.3	0.3
Bank	114,581	298,354	177,204	85,034	0.3	0.3	0.3	0.2
Other	41,688	113,107	67,888	35,289	0.1	0.1	0.1	0.1
New account	32,352	77,538	56,549	37,521	0.1%	0.1%	0.1%	0.1%
Personal information	24,361	72,017	44,100	24,629	0.1%	0.1%	0.1%	0.1%
Multiple types	31,596	90,119	58,232	34,500	0.1%	0.1%	0.1%	0.1%
Existing account	25,803	69,062	44,128	26,810	0.1	0.1	0.1	0.1
Other	15,316	45,742	31,161	18,412	0.0	0.0	0.1	0.0

Source: Bureau of Justice Statistics, National Crime Victimization Survey, Identity Theft Supplement, 2012.

Standard errors for table 7: Violent victimization, by age of victim and victim–offender relationship, 2003–2013

Victim–offender relationship	12–24	25–49	50–64	65 or older
Known	1.3%	1.3%	1.9%	3.7%
Domestic	0.8	1.0	1.4	2.4
Intimate partner	0.6	0.9	1.0	1.6
Immediate family	0.4	0.3	0.8	1.4
Other relative	0.3	0.3	0.5	1.2
Well-known/casual acquaintance	1.2	1.0	1.7	3.4
Stranger	1.2%	1.2%	1.8%	3.6%
Unknown	0.6%	0.6%	0.9%	1.8%
Average annual violent victimizations	203,451	212,820	94,794	31,657

Source: Bureau of Justice Statistics, National Crime Victimization Survey, 2003–2013.

Standard errors for table 8: Percent of violent victimization, by victim–offender relationship and age of victim, 2003–2013

Victim–offender relationship	12–24	25–49	50–64	65 or older
Total	0.9%	1.0%	0.5%	0.2%
Known	1.2%	1.1%	0.7%	0.2%
Domestic	1.4	1.6	0.9	0.3
Intimate partner	1.5	1.8	0.8	0.2
Immediate family	2.7	2.6	2.1	0.7
Other relative	3.4	3.4	2.4	1.1
Well-known/casual acquaintance	1.4	1.2	0.8	0.3
Stranger	1.2%	1.3%	0.8%	0.3%
Unknown	2.1%	2.1%	1.3%	0.5%

Source: Bureau of Justice Statistics, National Crime Victimization Survey, 2003–2013.

Standard errors for table 9: Rate of violent victimization, by age of victim and victim characteristics, 2003–2013

Demographic characteristic	12–24	25–49	50–64	65 or older
Sex				
Male	2.1	1.2	1.0	0.5
Female	1.9	1.1	0.9	0.4
Race/Hispanic origin				
White	2.0	1.1	0.8	0.3
Black	3.1	1.9	1.8	1.0
Hispanic/Latino	2.3	1.3	1.5	1.0
Other race	2.7	1.8	1.8	1.3
Two or more races	9.3	9.1	9.4	5.1
Marital status				
Never married	1.7	1.6	2.3	1.7
Married	3.1	0.7	0.6	0.3
Widowed	21.3	6.9	2.5	0.4
Divorced	23.5	2.8	2.1	1.6
Separated	25.8	6.3	5.0	5.3
Household composition				
Single, no children	5.2	2.3	2.0	0.6
Married, no children	4.4	1.2	0.7	0.3
With children	2.2	1.0	1.9	1.4
Other	2.0	1.4	1.1	0.6
Household ownership status				
Owned	1.7	0.8	0.7	0.3
Rented	2.5	1.7	2.1	1.0
No cash rent	9.2	5.3	6.5	1.9

Source: Bureau of Justice Statistics, National Crime Victimization Survey, 2003–2013.

Standard errors for table 10: Number and rate of violent victimization for persons age 65 or older, by type of crime and victim's disability status, 2008–2012

Type of crime	Number of violent victimizations		Rate per 1,000 persons	
	With disabilities	Without disabilities	With disabilities	Without disabilities
Total violent crime	47,909	69,450	0.7	0.6
Serious violent crime	26,853	29,152	0.4	0.2
Rape/sexual assault	16,552	7,135	0.2	0.1
Robbery	13,301	19,314	0.2	0.2
Aggravated assault	11,344	17,243	0.2	0.1
Simple assault	33,645	54,982	0.5	0.4

Source: Bureau of Justice Statistics, National Crime Victimization Survey, 2008–2012.

Standard errors for table 11: Rates of violent and property victimization, by employment status and age, 2003–2013

Employment status and age	Violent crime	Property crime
Employed		
12–64	0.3	0.5
65 or older	0.1	0.3
Not employed/retired		
12–64	0.4	0.8
65 or older	0.3	1.4

Source: Bureau of Justice Statistics, National Crime Victimization Survey, 2003–2013.

Standard errors for table 12: Percent of violent victimizations involving a weapon, by age of victim, 2003–2013

Type of weapon	12–24	25–49	50–64	65 or older
No weapon	1.2%	1.2%	1.8%	3.5%
Weapon	1.0%	1.0%	1.4%	2.8%
Firearm	0.5	0.5	0.8	1.8
Knife	0.5	0.5	0.7	1.3
Other	0.5	0.5	0.8	1.6
Type unknown	0.2	0.2	0.3	0.7
Don't know	0.5%	0.5%	0.9%	2.1%
Average annual violent victimizations	203,451	212,820	94,794	31,657

Source: Bureau of Justice Statistics, National Crime Victimization Survey, 2003–2013.

Standard errors for table 13: Percent of violent victimizations resulting in injury and medical treatment, by age of victim, 2003–2013

Type of injury and treatment	12–24	25–49	50–64	65 or older
Not injured	1.2%	1.1%	1.6%	2.9%
Injured	1.1%	1.0%	1.4%	2.7%
Serious injuries	0.5	0.4	0.6	1.1
Bruises or cuts	1.0	0.9	1.3	2.4
Other injuries	0.3	0.3	0.4	1.2
Treatment for injury				
No treatment	1.9%	2.0%	3.4%	7.7%
Any treatment	1.8	1.9	3.3	7.6
Treatment setting				
At the scene/home of victim, neighbor, or friend/other location	2.6%	2.6%	4.7%	10.9%
In doctor's office/hospital emergency room/overnight at hospital	2.7	2.7	4.8	10.9

Source: Bureau of Justice Statistics, National Crime Victimization Survey, 2003–2013.

APPENDIX TABLE 20
Standard errors for table 14: Percentage of victimizations reported to police, by type of crime and age, 2003–2013

Type of crime	12–24	25–49	50–64	65 or older
Violent crime	1.2%	1.3%	1.9%	3.7%
Serious violent crime	1.8	1.8	2.9	5.6
Rape/sexual assault	2.6	3.0	4.7	9.3
Robbery	2.6	2.4	3.9	6.3
Aggravated assault	1.7	1.6	2.6	6.2
Simple assault	1.3	1.4	2.1	4.3
Property crime	0.9%	0.5%	0.7%	1.0%
Household burglary	1.7	0.9	1.3	1.7
Motor vehicle theft	2.3	1.1	1.7	2.6
Theft	0.9	0.5	0.6	1.0

Source: Bureau of Justice Statistics, National Crime Victimization Survey, 2003–2013.

APPENDIX TABLE 21
Standard errors for table 15: Violent crime victims who received assistance from a victim service agency, by age of victim, 2003–2013

Type of crime	12–24	25–49	50–64	65 or older
Total	0.5%	0.7%	0.9%	2.1%
Serious violent crime	0.9	1.1	1.5	4.6
Simple assault	0.6	0.7	0.9	1.7

Source: Bureau of Justice Statistics, National Crime Victimization Survey, 2003–2013.

APPENDIX TABLE 22
Rate of violent and property victimization against the elderly, by type of crime and age, 2003–2013

Type of crime	65–74	75–84	85 or older
Total violent crime	5.1	2.2	1.1
Serious violent crime	1.6	0.9	0.7
Rape/sexual assault	0.3	0.0 !	0.1 !
Robbery	0.7	0.5	0.4!
Aggravated assault	0.6	0.3	0.2 !
Simple assault	3.5	1.3	0.3!
Total property crime	84.3	61.7	51.5
Household burglary	19.6	15.4	16.9
Motor vehicle theft	3.7	1.8	1.1
Theft	61.0	44.5	33.4

Note: Victimization rates are per 1,000 persons age 65 or older for violent crimes and per 1,000 households for property crimes. See appendix table 23 for standard errors.

! Interpret with caution. Estimate based on 10 or fewer sample cases, or coefficient of variation is greater than 50%.

Source: Bureau of Justice Statistics, National Crime Victimization Survey, 2003–2013.

APPENDIX TABLE 23
Standard errors for appendix table 22: Rate of violent and property victimization against the elderly, by type of crime and age, 2003–2013

Type of crime	65–74	75–84	85 or older
Total violent crime	0.5	0.4	0.4
Serious violent crime	0.2	0.2	0.3
Rape/sexual assault	0.1	0.0	0.1
Robbery	0.1	0.1	0.2
Aggravated assault	0.1	0.1	0.1
Simple assault	0.4	0.3	0.2
Total property crime	2.2	2.2	3.1
Household burglary	0.9	1.0	1.6
Motor vehicle theft	0.3	0.3	0.3
Theft	1.7	1.7	2.3

Source: Bureau of Justice Statistics, National Crime Victimization Survey, 2003–2013.